"All things are connected. Whatever befalls the earth,
befalls the children of the earth."
- Cree

"The whole world is a family."
- Maha Upanishad 6.71-75

"The believers, in their mutual love, mercy,
and compassion, are like one body. If any part of it suffers,
the whole body responds to it with wakefulness and fever."
- Prophet Muhammad (Peace Be Upon Him)

"Love your neighbor as yourself."
- Matthew 22:39 (the Bible, New Testament)

"And you shall love your neighbor as yourself."
- Leviticus 19:18 (Torah)

"Radiate boundless love towards the entire world —
above, below, and across — unhindered,
without ill will, without enmity."
- Buddha

"Recognize all humanity as one race"
- Guru Granth Sahib, Ang 611

Disclaimer

The information in this book was correct at the time of publication, but the Author does not assume any liability for loss or damage caused by errors or omissions. The short stories, all names, characters, and incidents portrayed within them are fictitious.
No identification with actual persons (living or deceased), places, buildings, and products is intended or should be inferred.

Cover Illustration Roka Studio

Copyright © 2024 Hibiscus & Honey Publishing Limited

All rights reserved. No part of this book may be reproduced or used in any manner without the prior written permission of the copyright owner, except for the use of brief quotations in a book review.

ISBN: 978-1-0690643-0-1

October 2024

This book belongs to

_____

_____

Sat Sri Akal!

Welcome to your exciting journey in the Sikhi Adventures series!
In this book, you'll explore the amazing story of Guru Angad Dev Ji!

Here's what's waiting for you inside:
- Meet Guru Angad Dev Ji!
- What is Gurmukhi? Learn about the script
- The Power of Seva and Humility
- Healthy Body, Healthy Mind
- Bonus Section - Something special just for you!

Let's dive in and explore the incredible legacy of Guru Angad Dev Ji together.
Your Sikhi Adventure starts now!

THE SECOND SIKH GURU
GURU ANGAD DEV JI

Meet Guru Angad Dev Ji

- Guru Angad Dev Ji, born as Bhai Lehna in 1504 in Matte-di-Sarai (now Sarai Naga), near Muktsar, Punjab, was curious and thoughtful from a young age. He loved learning and often listened to teachings from local priests.

- As Lehna grew, he helped with his family's business but felt drawn to something deeper. When he heard about Guru Nanak Dev Ji and his message of love and equality, Bhai Lehna knew he had to meet the Guru.

- That meeting changed everything. Inspired by Guru Nanak's teachings, Lehna became his follower, beginning a journey that would lead him to become the second Sikh Guru as Guru Angad Dev Ji.

HIDDEN CLUES ADVENTURE

Can you find the hidden objects in the picture of Guru Angad Dev Ji?

Look for:

A pen (for writing), kids jumping silhouette (for fitness and joy), and folded hands (for seva).

Circle them when you find them!

Guru Angad's Early Life

Bhai Lehna (later Guru Angad) was born to a loving family.

- His father, Baba Pheru Ji, was the village head, and his mother, Mata Ramo Ji, ensured that her children grew up in a religious and honest environment.

- Bhai Lehna was deeply spiritual and loved serving others. His natural leadership was evident even before meeting Guru Nanak, as he led groups of pilgrims to the temple.

- It was on one of these travels that Bhai Lehna heard a beautiful shabad by Guru Nanak Ji.

- He was so inspired by Guru Nanak's message that he began to want to meet the Guru. But little did he know that meeting Guru Nanak Dev Ji would change his life.

BHAI LEHNA JI'S JOURNEY TO GURU NANAK

Use the story you just read to answer each question by circling the best choice.

1. Bhai Lehna Ji grew up in a loving family. Who made sure he grew up in a religious and honest environment?
A) His father
B) His mother
C) His uncle

2. Even before meeting Guru Nanak, Bhai Lehna was a natural leader. What did he do to show his leadership?
A) Led groups of pilgrims to the temple
B) Taught kids how to read
C) Was the village head

3. What did Bhai Lehna hear that inspired him to want to meet Guru Nanak Dev Ji?
A) A painting
B) A shabad
C) A story

Meeting Guru Nanak Dev Ji

- The day had finally come when Bhai Lehna was about 30 years old. He learned that Guru Nanak Dev Ji was in a nearby town called Kartarpur. Excited and determined, Lehna set off to meet the Guru, eager to learn from him.

- Upon arriving at Kartarpur, Lehna felt a mix of nervousness and excitement. He had heard wonderful stories about Guru Nanak's teachings and the kindness he showed to everyone.

- When he finally met the Guru, he was welcomed with open arms and a warm smile. Guru Nanak spoke to Lehna about love, equality, and the importance of serving others. He taught him that all people are equal, regardless of their background.

- This message touched Lehna deeply and made him realize that he wanted to dedicate his life to these values by becoming a Sikh (student).

VALUES OF NANAK
WORD SEARCH

P	Y	A	A	R	K	Y	A	N	X	D	L	J
A	B	F	B	J	I	F	M	X	F	P	Y	E
E	K	T	A	L	S	V	V	V	D	M	O	R
L	R	X	R	K	A	K	J	V	E	Q	H	N
Z	C	Q	A	A	V	R	S	G	U	R	U	M
M	N	H	B	B	C	G	E	W	J	G	R	I
R	V	Z	A	C	H	I	V	M	I	O	T	G
A	B	O	R	D	C	N	A	M	G	T	L	M
B	W	H	I	U	S	I	K	H	Y	A	D	P
P	I	V	N	B	S	V	K	C	A	S	A	X
V	I	T	Q	F	E	P	V	X	S	J	Y	S
B	D	H	D	B	N	I	M	R	A	T	A	G
K	T	K	H	O	G	A	P	O	N	L	L	M

RAB
EKTA
SIKHYA
BARABARI

SEVA
PYAAR
NIMRATA

GURU
DAYAL
JIGYASA

Lessons from Guru Nanak

- Guru Angad Dev Ji dedicated himself to learning important lessons from Guru Nanak Dev Ji.

- One lesson was about the oneness of God (Ik Onkar). Guru Nanak taught that there is one God who loves everyone. This inspired Guru Angad to share this message, which you'll learn more about in the next section.

- Another lesson was about equality. Guru Nanak believed everyone should be treated the same, no matter their background or gender. Guru Angad promised to spread this idea to unite people.

- He also learned the value of humility. Guru Nanak showed that being kind is strong. He realized that by helping others, selflessly (seva), he was serving Waheguru. These teachings guided him as he became Guru Angad Dev Ji.

WORDS OF WISDOM

Draw a line to connect each teaching of Guru Nanak Dev Ji with its correct meaning.

PHRASE

1. "All people are equal."

2. "Serve others with love."

3. "Love is the greatest strength."

MEANING

A) Only some people are important.
B) Everyone deserves the same respect and kindness.

A) Help others only when you feel like it.
B) Always be kind and help others without expecting anything in return.

A) Being strong means never needing help.
B) When we love one another, we can make the world better.

Becoming the Second Guru

- Bhai Lehna spent 12 years in Guru Nanak Dev Ji's company, learning from him and serving him with devotion.

- Before Guru Nanak Dev Ji passed away, he tested Bhai Lehna's humility, dedication, and faith through several challenges.

- In one instance, Guru Nanak Dev Ji asked his sons and disciples to repair a broken house that had fallen, but only Bhai Lehna attempted it, showing his faith and willingness to serve.

- Impressed by Bhai Lehna's unwavering loyalty, selflessness and devotion, Guru Nanak Dev Ji passed the Gur-Gaddi (Divine Throne) to him.

  - During this time, because of Bhai Lehna's love for Guru Nanak he was given the name Guru Angad, meaning "a part of the Guru".

Recap: Important Lessons

- After Guru Nanak Dev Ji, Guru Angad Dev Ji was appointed as the second Guru of the Sikhs.

- Guru Angad Dev Ji embraced his new role with full understanding of the responsibility to guide and care for the growing Sikh community.

- He became a living example of Guru Nanak's values—through his actions, he demonstrated how to live with kindness, help others, and treat everyone with fairness.

- Guru Angad Dev Ji also emphasized the importance of understanding and practicing Guru Nanak Dev Ji's teachings, especially the message of Ik Onkar (One Creator).

- He showed that spiritual growth comes from applying these teachings in everyday life.

GURU ANGAD DEV JI'S JOURNEY RECAP

Answer each question by circling the correct choice!

1. Who was appointed as the second Guru of the Sikhs after Guru Nanak Dev Ji?
A) Guru Gobind Singh Ji
B) Guru Angad Dev Ji
C) Guru Amar Das Ji

2. What are some of the core values that Guru Angad Dev Ji demonstrated?
A) Humility, equality, and seva (selfless service)
B) Wealth and power
C) Fear and anger

3. What did Guru Angad Dev Ji teach about the importance of Guru Nanak Dev Ji's teachings?
A) They should be ignored
B) They are only for special people
C) They should be understood and practiced in daily life

4. What does "Ik Onkar" mean?
A) Many gods
B) One Creator
C) No creator

This section has lots of fun coloring pages just for you! Use crayons or colored pencils to make sure the colors don't go through the pages. Have fun coloring your masterpiece!

GURMUKHI

The Creation of Gurmukhi

- Before Guru Angad Dev Ji's time, people in India used many different languages and scripts for writing, especially for religious books.

- Some used Sanskrit, a very old language that only scholars and priests knew. Others used Persian and Arabic, which were the languages of the rulers and the powerful.

- Most people in Punjab spoke Punjabi, but there wasn't a standard way to write it, and this was made worse because many people couldn't read or write at all.

- Since people couldn't write in their own language, it was difficult for them to learn the teachings of Guru Nanak Dev Ji.

- Guru Angad Dev Ji wanted to change this so that everyone could learn. So, he developed Gurmukhi.

Importance of Learning Gurmukhi

- Guru Angad Dev Ji encouraged people to learn Gurmukhi so they could read and understand the teachings of the Guru Nanak.

- He believed that <u>education is important for everyone, both young and old</u>. By learning to read and write in Gurmukhi, people could connect more deeply with Sikh teachings and grow on their spiritual journey.

- Guru Angad Dev Ji set up classes and taught both children and adults the Gurmukhi script. He showed that everyone should have the chance to learn and that education is for all, not just a select few.

DESIGN YOUR CLASS
Draw your Gurmukhi classroom where kids and adults come to learn.

GURMUKHI LEARNING PATH

In this adventure you'll meet the first three letters of the Gurmukhi alphabet: ੳ *(Ura),* ਅ *(Aira), and* ੲ *(Iri).*

Each letter makes its own sound. Here's how they work:

ੳ (Ura): This letter makes the "U" sound, like in the words "put" or "push."

ਅ (Aira): This one sounds like the "A" in "apple" or "amrit." It's the short, clear "A" sound we use at the beginning of many Punjabi words.

ੲ (Iri): This letter makes the "I" sound, like in "sit" or "ink." It helps form lots of words you might know, like "Ik" (meaning one).

Now that we know how these letters sound, it's time to practice! On the next three pages follow the dotted lines. Don't worry if it's tricky at first – practice is the key!

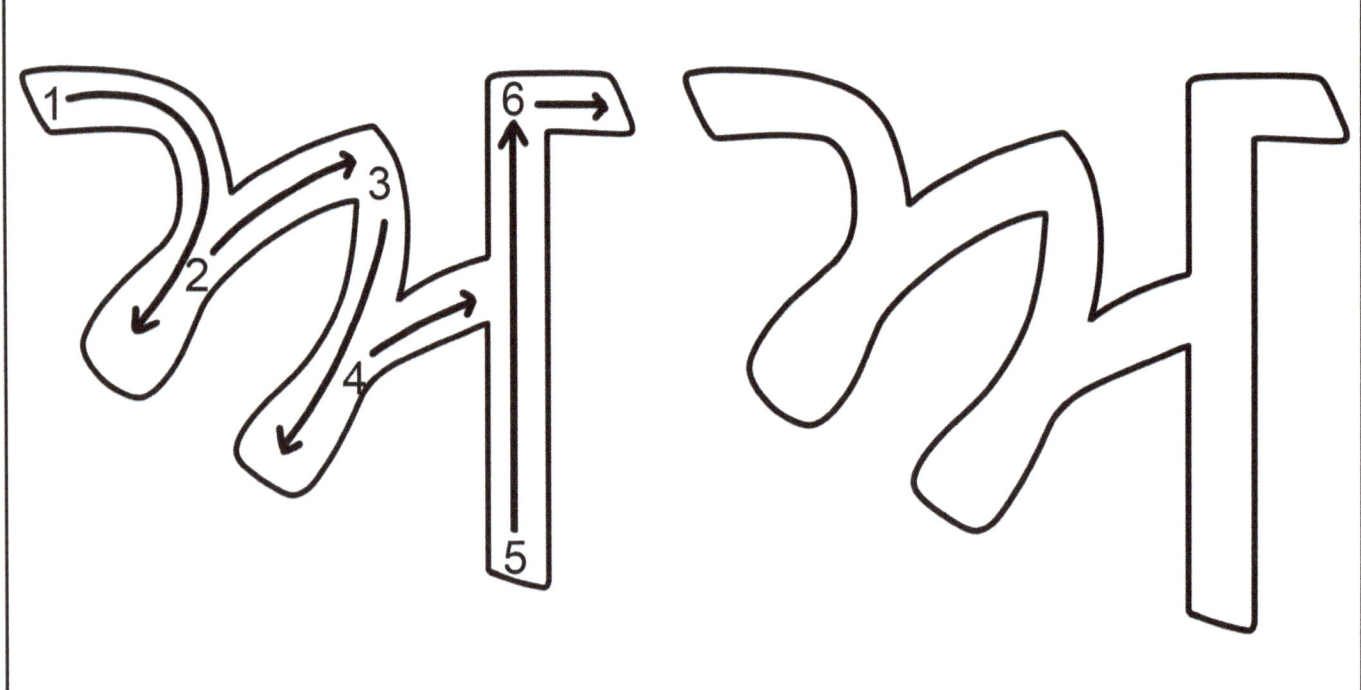

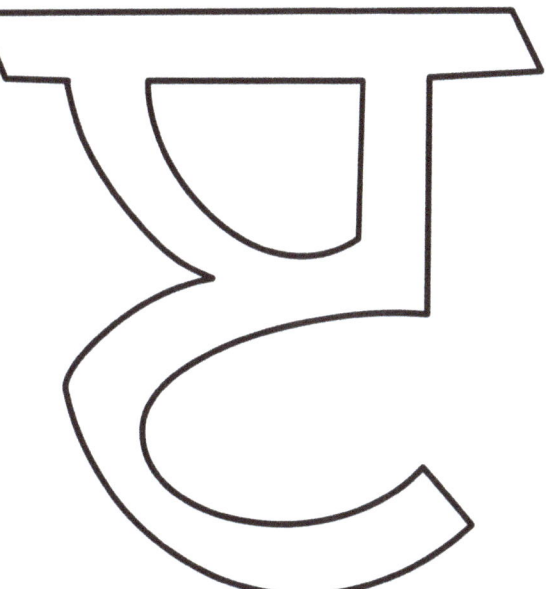

This section has lots of fun coloring pages just for you! Continue to use crayons or colored pencils to make sure the colors don't go through the pages.

SELFLESS ACTION

Seva: The Gift of Helping Others

- Guru Angad Dev Ji taught that one of the most important things in life is seva—helping others without expecting anything in return.

- Seva is not just a good thing to do, it's a way to connect with Waheguru and the people around us. When we help others, we are also serving God.

- Before Guru Angad Dev Ji's time, helping others was often based on social status.

- Rich people mostly helped other rich people, and poor people were often left out. Some jobs were seen as only for certain people, while others were not treated equally.

- But Guru Angad Dev Ji believed everyone, no matter how rich or poor, should help and serve others.

SEVA IN ACTION

Let's think about how we can practice seva in our everyday lives, just like Guru Angad Dev Ji taught! Below are different examples of ways you can help others. **Circle the ones that you think show true seva**—helping without expecting anything in return!

1) Helping clean up the park with your family, even though no one asked.

2) Giving water to someone who is thirsty without being told to do so.

3) Cleaning up your room after being told by your parents.

4) Donating your toys to kids who don't have any.

5) Helping your sibling clean up a mess even if it wasn't yours.

6) Only helping out when you know you'll get a reward.

Seva: The Gift of Helping Others Cont'd

- Guru Angad Dev Ji set an example by doing seva himself. He swept floors, cleaned the kitchen, and served food to people—rich or poor, young or old. This showed that no job was too small when it came to helping others.

- He encouraged everyone to take part in Langar, the free community kitchen started by Guru Nanak Dev Ji.

- In Langar, everyone sits together and eats the same food, showing that all people are equal. Helping in the Langar, by cooking, cleaning, or serving food, is a special way to practice seva.

- Guru Angad Dev Ji believed that true seva came from humility—being humble. He taught that when we help others, we should do it with a kind heart, without expecting praise or rewards.

- This kind of seva brings us closer to Waheguru and makes our community stronger.

TAKING ACTION IN YOUR OWN LIFE

Write a short paragraph (3-4 sentences) about how you can apply one of Guru Angad Dev Ji's teachings—like kindness or helping others—in your own life.

This section has lots of fun coloring pages just for you! Use crayons or colored pencils to make sure the colors don't go through the pages. Have fun coloring your masterpiece!

LANGAR

The Power of Langar

- Following Guru Nanak Dev Ji's example, Guru Angad Dev Ji made Langar a key part of life to show that everyone is equal.

- In Langar, rich or poor, men or women, young or old—all sit together and eat the same food, with no differences between them.

- He taught that sharing food shows love and respect. Eating together builds friendships and strengthens community, reminding us we are all one big family.

- Every day, volunteers cooked and served simple meals like roti, dal, and sabji. The power of Langar lies not just in the food, but in the love and friendship it creates.

FILL IN THE BLANKS

Use the words below to complete the sentences about the important lessons Guru Ji shared through Langar

MONEY   LOVE   FRIENDSHIP   RESPECT
TOGETHER   ROTI   DAL   SABJI

1) In Langar, everyone sits _____ and eats the same food.

2) Sharing food shows _____ and _____.

3) Volunteers cooked and served simple meals like _____, _____, and _____.

4) Langar teaches us that helping others is more important than _____. (Hint: Rich or Poor)

5) The power of Langar is not just in the food, but in the love and _____ it creates.

Guru Angad's Biggest Supporter

Mata Khivi Ji, was the wife of Guru Angad Dev Ji, and was known for her kindness and strong character. She supported Guru Ji and the Sikh community in many ways.

For example, Mata Khivi Ji made sure the kitchen was organized and that everyone, no matter who they were, received healthy meals <u>with kindness and respect</u>. Mata Khivi Ji helped prepare and serve food, always welcoming visitors and making them feel at home.

She also encouraged others to join in and help with Langar, teaching everyone about the values of equality and helping one another. Her hard work helped bring the Sikh community together, making Langar a special place where everyone could share a meal as equals.

MATA KHIVI'S KINDNESS

Inspired by Mata Khivi Ji's example of kindness and helping others, complete the sentences below with your own ideas!

1) Write or draw one way you can help others and show kindness and respect, just like Mata Khivi Ji!

2) Why is it important to be kind and respectful to others?

3) Write one sentence about how can we work together in our community, like Mata Khivi Ji did?

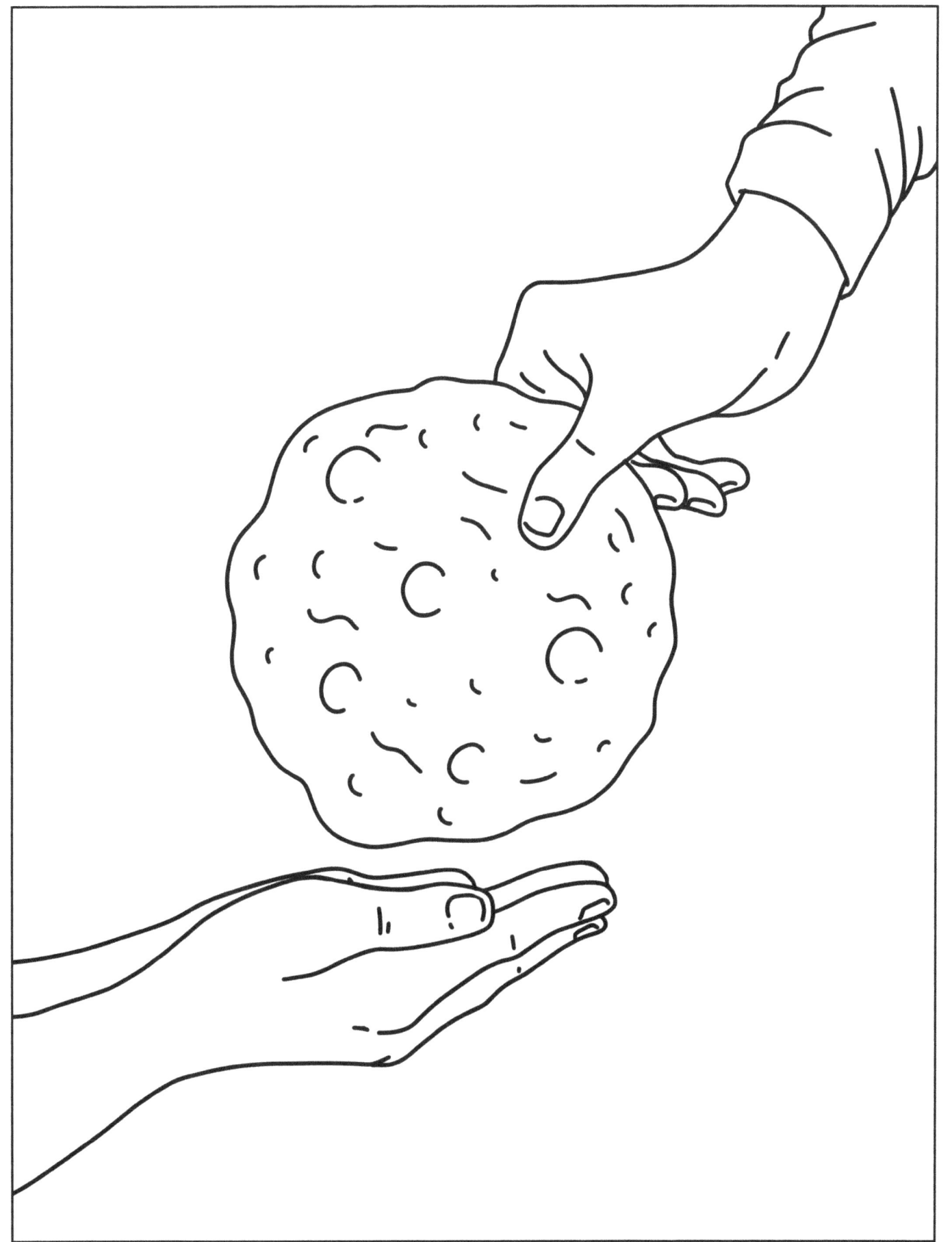

This section has lots of fun coloring pages just for you! Use crayons or colored pencils to make sure the colors don't go through the pages. Have fun coloring your masterpiece!

PLAY TIME

Strong Body, Strong Mind

🟩 Guru Angad Dev Ji emphasized the importance of maintaining both a strong body and mind.

🟩 He believed that regular exercise keeps us healthy and ready to serve others.

🟩 To promote this, he established Mal Akhara (wrestling ground) where Sikhs could train and build physical strength.

TRUE OR FALSE

Circle whether each sentence is "True" or "False":

1) Guru Angad Dev Ji taught the importance of regular exercise.	TRUE/FALSE
2) The Mal Akhara was a place for playing board games.	TRUE/FALSE
3) Exercising only helps the body, not the mind.	TRUE/FALSE
4) Guru Angad Dev Ji believed that fitness was a way to prepare for selfless service.	TRUE/FALSE

FUN ACTIVITIES
WORD SEARCH

```
A V R U N U E K R Y S L
W K D A N C E X U T U V
C I S H S L I T U W W O
U E T S W I M V B U W K
C Z R J U M P W I P U P
H W E P E B T F K L O P
K M T B S K A T E A I K
O U C G Q K D D B Y N Y
Q I H I K E O H K O T C
H K X G Z Z V M U G F W
N Q T P B M Q P I A U S
V C E W A L K Z K Z N S
```

RUN	JUMP	PLAY
BIKE	SWIM	YOGA
WALK	HIKE	DANCE
SKATE	CLIMB	STRETCH

Basketball

Soccer

Jump Rope

Karate

Activities with Friends!

- The Mal Akhara was more than just a place to exercise—it was a way for people to come together, work hard, and become stronger as a community.

- People trained in wrestling, running, and other forms of exercise. This helped them stay focused and healthy to better serve others through seva.

CREATE YOUR OWN ROUTINE

Let's create our own fun activity routine, just like in Guru Ji's Mal Akhara. Write down three exercises you enjoy that make you strong, fast, and healthy! Then try them out with friends! Examples: jumping jacks (10 reps), running in place (1 minute), push-ups (5 reps).

1)

2)

3)

Balance Your Body and Mind

- Guru Angad Dev Ji taught that exercise wasn't just about being strong physically—it also helped clear the mind.
- When we exercise, we feel better, think more clearly, and are more prepared to help others. Taking care of both your body and mind is a way to show love to yourself and thanks for the life you have.

FITNESS CHALLENGE: BODY & MIND

Find a friend or family member to do this fitness challenge with! Take turns leading each other through these exercises. How many can you do? Write your results below!

ACTIVITIES	RESULTS #1	RESULTS #2
1) Star Jumps – How many can you do in 30 seconds?		
2) Hop like a frog across the room. How many hops can you do in 1 minute?		
3) Breathing Exercise – Sit quietly for 1 minute and take slow, deep breaths. How does your body feel?		

REFLECTION

Imagine Meeting Guru Angad Dev Ji

- Close your eyes and imagine you are meeting Guru Angad Dev Ji. He welcomes you with a warm smile.

- What do you think it would be like to sit with him and talk? Maybe you'd share stories, ask him questions, or tell him how his teachings have helped you.

- Think about how his words and actions have inspired you. Would you thank him for developing Gurmukhi, or for reminding us to stay strong and help others?

WRITE A LETTER TO GURU ANGAD DEV JI

This is your chance to express your feelings to him, just like you would to a wise friend.

Now, take a moment to write down what you would say to him. Your letter can be about anything! From what you admire about him, to questions you might have, or how you want to live by his example.

Dear Guru Angad Dev Ji,

With love and respect,

FRIENDLY QUIZ

Test Your Knowledge!

1. What script did Guru Angad Dev Ji help develop?
a) Devanagari
b) Gurmukhi
c) Arabic
d) Latin

2. Which important value did Guru Angad Dev Ji promote?
a) Wealth
b) Competition
c) Seva (selfless service)
d) Fame

3. What kind of physical activity did Guru Angad Dev Ji encourage Sikhs to practice?
a) Sleeping
b) Wrestling
c) Chess
d) Meditating

Short Answer Quiz: Discovering Guru Angad Dev Ji

Answer the questions below in complete sentences.

1) What was Guru Angad Dev Ji's name before becoming a Guru?

2) Name one contribution Guru Angad Dev Ji made to the Sikh community.

3) Why did Guru Angad Dev Ji believe physical fitness was important?

4) What is a lesson you can learn from Guru Angad Dev Ji's life?

Glossory Adventure: Discovering Meaningful Words on Our Journey

Rab	God
Ekta	Unity
Sikhya	Teachings
Barabari	Equality
Seva	Selfless Service
Pyaar	Love
Nimrata	Humility
Guru	Spiritual Teacher
Dayal	Compassionate
Jigyasa	Curiousity

ANSWER SHEETS

HIDDEN CLUES ADVENTURE

Look for:
A pen ✒ (for writing), kids jumping silhouette 🕺 (for fitness and joy), and folded hands 🤲 (for seva).

BHAI LEHNA'S JOURNEY TO GURU NANAK

1. B) His mother
2. A) Led groups of pilgrims to the temple
3. B) A shabad

Values of Nanak Word Search

P	Y	A	A	R	K	Y	A	N	X	D	L	J
A	B	F	B	J	I	F	M	X	F	P	Y	E
E	K	T	A	L	S	V	V	V	D	M	O	R
L	R	X	R	K	A	K	J	V	E	Q	H	N
Z	C	Q	A	A	V	R	S	G	U	R	U	M
M	N	H	B	B	C	G	E	W	J	G	R	I
R	V	Z	A	C	H	I	V	M	I	O	T	G
A	B	O	R	D	C	N	A	M	G	T	L	M
B	W	H	I	U	S	I	K	H	Y	A	D	P
P	I	V	N	B	S	V	K	C	A	S	A	X
V	I	T	Q	F	E	P	V	X	S	J	Y	S
B	D	H	D	B	N	I	M	R	A	T	A	G
K	T	K	H	O	G	A	P	O	N	L	L	M

RAB	SEVA	GURU
EKTA	PYAAR	DAYAL
SIKHYA	NIMRATA	JIGYASA
BARABARI		

WORDS OF WISDOM

1. "All people are equal."
   A) Only some people are important.
   B) Everyone deserves the same respect and kindness.

2. "Serve others with love."
   A) Help others only when you feel like it.
   B) Always be kind and help others without expecting anything in return.

3. "Love is the greatest strength."
   A) Being strong means never needing help.
   B) When we love one another, we can make the world better.

GURU ANGAD DEV JI'S JOURNEY RECAP

1. B) Guru Angad Dev Ji
2. A) Humility, equality, and seva (selfless service)
3. C) They should be understood and practiced in daily life
4. B) One Creator

SEVA IN ACTION

1) Helping clean up the park with your family, even though no one asked.

2) Giving water to someone who is thirsty without being told to do so.

4) Donating your toys to kids who don't have any.

5) Helping your sibling clean up a mess even if it wasn't yours.

FILL IN THE BLANKS

1) TOGETHER
3) ROTI/DAL/SABJI
5) FRIENDSHIP

2) LOVE AND RESPECT
4) MONEY

TRUE OR FALSE

1) TRUE
2) FALSE
3) FALSE
4) TRUE

Fun Activities Word Search

A	V	R	U	N	U	E	K	R	Y	S	L
W	K	D	A	N	C	E	X	U	T	U	V
C	I	S	H	S	L	I	T	U	W	W	O
U	E	T	S	W	I	M	V	B	U	W	K
C	Z	R	J	U	M	P	W	I	P	U	P
H	W	E	P	E	B	T	F	K	L	O	P
K	M	T	B	S	K	A	T	E	A	I	K
O	U	C	G	Q	K	D	D	B	Y	N	Y
Q	I	H	I	K	E	O	H	K	O	T	C
H	K	X	G	Z	Z	V	M	U	G	F	W
N	Q	T	P	B	M	Q	P	I	A	U	S
V	C	E	W	A	L	K	Z	K	Z	N	S

Friendly Quiz - Test Your Knowledge!

1. What script did Guru Angad Dev Ji help develop?
b) Gurmukhi

2. Which important value did Guru Angad Dev Ji promote?
c) Seva (selfless service)

3. What kind of physical activity did Guru Angad Dev Ji encourage Sikhs to practice?
b) Wrestling

Short Answer Quiz: Discovering Guru Angad Dev Ji

1) What was Guru Angad Dev Ji's name before becoming a Guru?
Answer: Bhai Lehna

2) Name **one** contribution Guru Angad Dev Ji made to the Sikh community.
Possible responses: Seva, Gurmukhi, Physical Fitness, Langar

3) Why did Guru Angad Dev Ji believe physical fitness was important? Suggested: Because he taught that being strong and healthy allows one to perform seva more effectively, live with discipline, and stay focused on spiritual growth.

4) What is a lesson you can learn from Guru Angad Dev Ji's life?
Suggested: the importance of humility and serving others selflessly.

BONUS

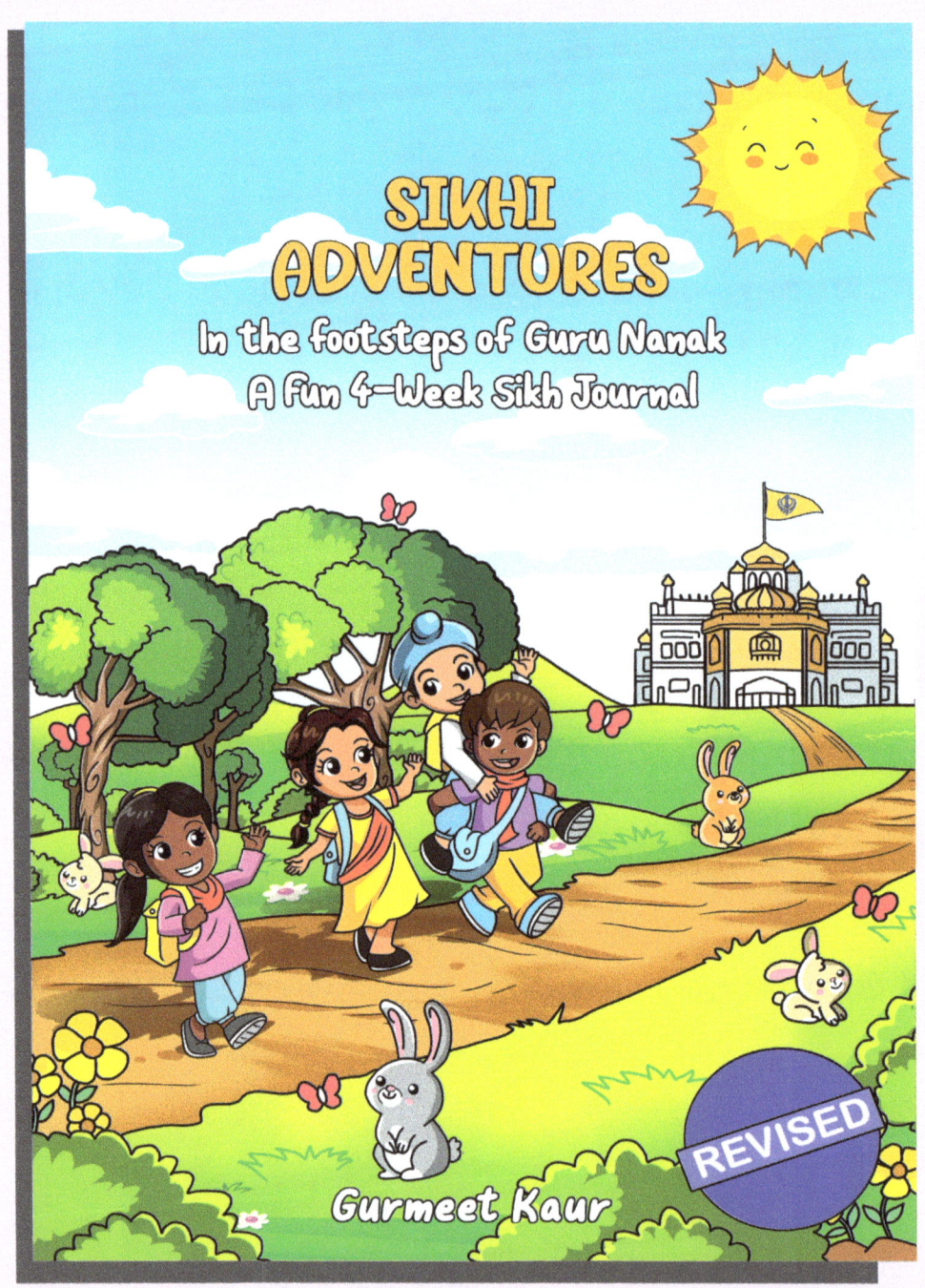

JOURNAL PREVIEW

Guru Nanak's Principles

Naam Japo
Remembering Waheguru through meditation

Kirat Karo
Perform work honestly to earn your living

Vand Ke Chakko
Share your honest earnings with those in need

Date:

Naam Japna (Meditation or Prayer)

How many minutes did you spend in meditation or prayer today?

- [ ] 0-5 minutes
- [ ] 6-10 minutes
- [ ] 11-15 minutes
- [ ] 16+ minutes

Kirat Karni (Honest Living)

What is one honest or helpful thing you did today?

- [ ] Completed homework
- [ ] Shared with others
- [ ] Helped a friend
- [ ] Told the truth even if it was hard

Vand Ke Chhako (Sharing with Others)

How did you share or help others today?

- [ ] Helped a family member
- [ ] Shared snacks
- [ ] Did a chore without being asked
- [ ] Volunteered
- [ ] Something else:

Draw or write about your favourite moment with your sibling or friend

Date:

Naam Japna (Meditation or Prayer)

How many minutes did you spend in meditation or prayer today?

- [ ] 0-5 minutes
- [ ] 6-10 minutes
- [ ] 11-15 minutes
- [ ] 16+ minutes

Kirat Karni (Honest Living)

What is one honest or helpful thing you did today?

- [ ] Completed homework
- [ ] Shared with others
- [ ] Helped a friend
- [ ] Told the truth even if it was hard

Vand Ke Chhako (Sharing with Others)

How did you share or help others today?

- [ ] Helped a family member
- [ ] Shared snacks
- [ ] Did a chore without being asked
- [ ] Volunteered
- [ ] Something else:

Draw or write about something you did today that was really hard

Pavan Guru

Air is the Guru

Pani Pita

Water is the Father

Mata Dharat Mahat

And the beloved Earth,
the greatest Mother of all